D0306498

A Tiny Teddy

Poems about Toys

Chosen by John Foster

OXFORD
UNIVERSITY PRESS

OXFORD

UNIVERSITY PRESS

Great Clarendon Street, Oxford OX2 6DP

Oxford University Press is a department of the University of Oxford.
It furthers the University's objective of excellence in research, scholarship,
and education by publishing worldwide in

Oxford New York

Athens Auckland Bangkok Bogotá Buenos Aires
Cape Town Chennai Dar es Salaam Delhi Florence Hong Kong Istanbul
Karachi Kolkata Kuala Lumpur Madrid Melbourne Mexico City Mumbai
Nairobi Paris São Paulo Shanghai Singapore Taipei Tokyo Toronto
Warsaw

with associated companies in Berlin Ibadan

Oxford is a registered trade mark of Oxford University Press
in the UK and in certain other countries

Copyright © John Foster 2001
Originally published as I'm Riding on a Giant © John Foster 1999 and
A Teeny Tiny Teddy © John Foster 1999

The moral rights of the author have been asserted

Database right Oxford University Press (maker)

First published in this edition 2001

All rights reserved. No part of this publication may be reproduced,
stored in a retrieval system, or transmitted, in any form or by any means,
without the prior permission in writing of Oxford University Press.
Within the UK, exceptions are allowed in respect of any fair
dealing for the purpose of research or private study, or criticism or
review, as permitted under the Copyright, Designs and Patents Act 1988,
or in the case of reprographic reproduction in accordance with
the terms of the licences issued by the Copyright Licensing Agency.
Enquiries concerning reproduction outside these terms and in other
countries should be sent to the Rights Department, Oxford University Press,
at the address above.

This book is sold subject to the condition that it shall not, by way of trade or
otherwise, be lent, re-sold, hired out or otherwise circulated without the
publisher's prior consent in any form of binding or cover other than that in
which it is published and without a similar condition including this
condition being imposed on the subsequent purchaser.

British Library Cataloguing in Publication Data available

ISBN 0 19 276288 5

10 9 8 7 6 5 4 3 2 1

Printed in China

We are grateful to the authors for permission to reprint the following poems.

First published in John Foster (ed.): *A Teeny Tiny Teddy* (OUP, 1999):
Gina Douthwaite: 'Riding on My Rocking Horse', © Gina Douthwaite 1999;
John Foster: 'There's a Dragon in the Sky', © John Foster 1999; **Robin
Mellor:** 'In Our Bath', © Robin Mellor 1999; **Trevor Millum:** 'What's in the
Box?', © Trevor Millum 1999; **Tony Mitton:** 'Working My Robot', © Tony
Mitton 1999; **Marian Swinger:** 'A Teeny Tiny Teddy', © Marian Swinger
1999; **Celia Warren:** 'Squeals on Wheels', © Celia Warren 1999.

First published in John Foster (ed.): *I'm Riding on a Giant* (OUP, 1999):

Faustin Charles: 'The Land of No Grown-ups', © Faustin Charles 1999;
John Foster: 'My Big Cardboard Box', © John Foster 1999; **Tony Mitton:**
'My Bed', © Tony Mitton 1999; **Cynthia Rider:** 'Sea-Shell', © Cynthia Rider
1999; **David Whitehead:** 'I'm Riding on a Giant', © David Whitehead 1999.

We are also grateful for permission to reprint the following poems:

Finola Akister: 'My Roller Skates' and 'If I Could Choose' from *Before I Grow
Up* (Viking Kestrel, 1987), copyright © Finola Akister 1987, reprinted by
permission of Penguin Books Ltd; **Lucy Coates:** 'O My Grand Old Grandpa
York' from *First Rhymes* (1994), by permission of the publisher, Orchard
Books, a division of the Watts Publishing Group, 96 Leonard Street, London
EC2A 4RH; **Wendy Cope:** 'My Old Guitar' from *Twiddling Your Thumbs*,
reprinted by permission of the publishers, Faber & Faber Ltd; **Richard
Edwards:** 'If I Wore Shining Armour' from *If Only*, © Richard Edwards 1990,
reprinted by permission of the author; **Ann Marie Linden:** 'Wishes' first
published in *Steel Drums* (BBC Books), reprinted by permission of the author.

Despite efforts to obtain permission from all copyright holders before
publication, this has not been possible in a few cases. If notified the
publisher will be pleased to rectify any errors or omissions at the earliest
opportunity.

KNOWSLEY SCHOOL
LIBRARY SERVICE

PROJECT LOAN
20623728

The illustrations are by:
Ivan Bates pp. 12–13; Annabel Collis pp. 16–17; Kelly Dooley pp. 6–7;
Serena Feneziano pp. 4–5, 30–31; Janice Gelineau pp. 19, 20–21; Rebecca
Gryspeerdt p. 28; Charlotte Hard pp. 14–15, 29; Anthony Lewis pp. 8–9,
22–23; Valerie McBride p. 18;
Jo Moore p. 11; Liz Pichon pp. 10, 24–25; Kay Widdowson pp. 26–27, 32

List of contents:

The Land of No Grown-Ups	*Faustin Charles*	4
What's in the Box?	*Trevor Millum*	6
A Teeny Tiny Teddy	*Marian Swinger*	8
There's a Dragon in the Sky	*John Foster*	10
Working My Robot	*Tony Mitton*	11
A Good Play	*Robert Louis Stevenson*	12
Squeals on Wheels	*Celia Warren*	14
My Roller Skates	*Finola Akister*	15
My Big Cardboard Box	*John Foster*	16
If I wore Shining Armour	*Richard Edwards*	18
Riding on My Rocking Horse	*Gina Douthwaite*	19
Sea-Shell	*Cynthia Rider*	20
Miss Polly	*Anon*	22
In Our Bath	*Robin Mellor*	24
O My Grand Old Grandpa York	*Lucy Coats*	25
Wishes	*Ann Marie Linden*	26
If I Could Choose	*Finola Akister*	28
My Old Guitar	*Wendy Cope*	29
I'm Riding on a Giant	*David Whitehead*	30
My Bed	*Tony Mitton*	32

The Land of No Grown-ups

In the land of no grown-ups,
Playing never stops:
With a play, play here,
And a play, play there,
Children playing everywhere,
The playing never stops,
In the land of no grown-ups,
You can eat ice-cream all day,
No one will take it away,
So the eating never stops,
In the land of no grown-ups.

In the land of no grown-ups,
You can have your own way,
There is no one to say,
That's all for today,
In the land of no-grown-ups.

Faustin Charles

What's in the Box?

What's in the toy box?
What's in the box?
What's in the box
With the big brass locks?

There's a one-eyed ted
And a ball that's red,
Some building bricks
And a clock that ticks,
A plastic boat
And a duck that floats,
A wind-up car
And a silver star,
A doll that cries
And a plane that flies.

That's what's in the toy box!
That's what's in the box!

Trevor Millum

A Teeny Tiny Teddy

A tiny teddy tottered
as she tap danced to and fro.
A tubby teddy tittered
as she teetered on a toe.

"Don't twizzle," said the teddy.
"Don't you tiptoe, twirl or tilt;
for teddies tend to totter;
that's the way that we are built.
Try tootling on my trumpet;
try my tuba or trombone.
It takes a Ted to tootle out
a truly terrific tone."

OOPS!

The tiny teddy twirled and twizzled,
tottered, teetered, tripped,
twittering as she twizzled
twirling as she tipped
and tumbled in the tuba
with a teeny tiny shout.
The tubby teddy tittered,
tootled hard, and blew her out.

Marian Swinger

Wheee!

There's a Dragon in the Sky

There's a dragon in the sky
Watch it dive and swoop!
See it shake its snaky tail
As it loops the loop.

There's a dragon in the sky.
I painted it bright red.
I made it with my Grandpa
In his garden shed.

There's a dragon in the sky,
Dancing, flying free.
There's a dragon in the sky
And it belongs to me.

John Foster

Working My Robot

When I press this button
my robot starts to talk.
When I press this button
my robot starts to walk.

When I pull this lever
he starts to turn around.
When I pull this lever
he makes a bleeping sound.

When I click this little switch
his lights begin to flash.
Oh! He's falling over…
Clink! Clank! Crash!

Tony Mitton

A Good Play

We built a ship upon the stairs
All made of the back-bedroom chairs,
And filled it full of sofa pillows
To go a-sailing on the billows.

We took a saw and several nails,
And water in the nursery pails;
And Tom said, "Let us also take
An apple and a slice of cake";
Which was enough for Tom and me
To go a-sailing on, till tea.

We sailed along for days and days,
And had the very best of plays;
But Tom fell out and hurt his knee,
So there was no one left but me.

Robert Louis Stevenson

Squeals on Wheels

Kate on a skateboard
skids to the gate,
spins to a standstill
   just too late,
falls off her skateboard –
   bad luck Kate:
hits her head
on the garden gate.

Raj in roller-boots
scoots to the door,
turning his toes in
   more and more,
trips in his roller-boots –
   Raj is sore:
bumps his bottom
on the concrete floor.

Celia Warren

My Roller Skates

My roller skates won't ever do
The simple things I want them to.
I put them on and try my best,
But one goes East and the other goes West.

I often fall upon the floor,
Then, full of pluck, I try once more.
But my roller skates think they know best:
One still goes East and the other West.

Finola Akister

My Big Cardboard Box

My big cardboard box is a tall sailing ship
That skims across the foam.
I load it with treasure from pirate wrecks
Before I head for home.

My big cardboard box is a silver rocket
That takes me to the stars.
I race through space to set up a base
And explore the surface of Mars.

My big cardboard box is a huge aeroplane.
I fly to golden sands,
Where lollipop trees and ice-cream flowers
Grow in a magic land.

There's nothing like a big cardboard box
To take you far away,
When you're stuck inside with nothing to do
On a wet and windy day.

John Foster

If I Wore Shining Armour

If I wore shining armour
Like knights of long ago,
I'd ride out after breakfast
Cross streams, cross fields of snow,
Climb wild enchanted mountains,
Chop off a dragon's head,
Ride home through wolf-filled forests
And be back in time for bed.

Richard Edwards

Riding on My Rocking Horse

Riding on my rocking horse,
trotting up and down,
jumping through the window,
galloping out of town,
flying off to see the sun,
meeting with the moon,
smiling wider every mile,
coming home soon…

riding,
trotting,
jumping,
galloping,
flying, meeting,
smiling,
coming
home
soon…

Gina Douthwaite

Sea-Shell

Sea-shell, sea-shell,
Whisper to me.
Whisper the secrets
Of the sea.

In faraway places
In faraway lands,
There are swaying palm-trees
And golden sands.

There are silvery mermaids
Who swim through the waves
And who dance and sing
In coral caves.

There are chests of treasure
And pirates' gold
Down on the ocean bed
Dark and cold.

These are the secrets
I can hear
With the whispering sea-shell
Close to my ear.

Cynthia Rider

Miss Polly

Miss Polly had a dolly
Who was sick, sick, sick,
So she called for the doctor
To come quick, quick, quick.

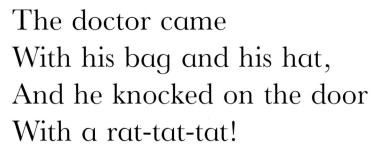

The doctor came
With his bag and his hat,
And he knocked on the door
With a rat-tat-tat!

He looked at the dolly
And he shook his head,
He said, "Miss Polly,
Put her straight to bed."

He wrote on a paper
For a pill, pill, pill.
"I'll be back in the morning
With my bill, bill, bill."

Anon

In Our Bath

In our bath is a wind-up hippo,
a purple duck and a rubber pillow,
a bar of soap in the shape of a fish
that floats on the water in a plastic dish;
there's a boat with a flapping paper sail
and a squashy sponge that squirts like a whale;
there are toys in the bath as far as you can see,
and just enough room for one little me!

Robin Mellor

O My Grand Old Grandpa York

O My Grand Old Grandpa York
He had ten thousand teds,
He marched them into their baths every night,
Then he marched them to their beds.
And when they got in they were wet,
And when they got out they were dry,
And when they were all snuggled up very tight
He sang them a lullaby.

Lucy Coats

Wishes

I'd like to hug
The lions in the zoo

And speckle my house
Green, yellow and blue,

And swim in a pool
Of orange that's

fizzy

And spin on the roundabouts
Without getting *dizzy*

And own a forever-chocolate cake
(That doesn't give you a stomach-ache),

And a bed that keeps you wide-awake
Until Father Christmas comes.

Ann Marie Linden

27

If I Could Choose

If I could choose
What I would be,
I'd like to be a bumble bee.
I'd bumble in and out of flowers,
But only during sunny hours,
For if it rained hard, you can bet
I'd bumble off and not get wet.

Finola Akister

My Old Guitar

I like to play my old guitar,
Strum, strum, strum –
Sometimes with my fingers,
Sometimes with my thumb.

I like to sit around and sing,
And dream that I'm a star.
I like to sit and sing and dream
And play my old guitar.

Wendy Cope

I'm Riding on a Giant

I'm riding on a giant.
I'm way up in the sky.
Looking down on everyone
From higher up than high.

I'm holding tight to giant's ears
As we stride along the street
Shouting down at people,
Hey! mind my giant's feet!

We're ducking down through doorways.
We're walking over walls.
I'm safe as houses way up here
My giant never falls.

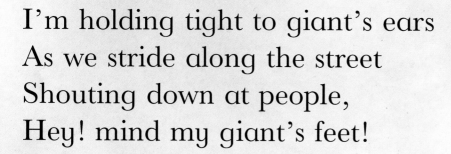

People down below us
Simply stop and stare.
Then when they see our shadow,
Oh wow! They get a scare.

I'm taller than the tree-tops
I'm high enough to fly.
Another centimetre and I'd
Bump into the sky.

I've been riding on my giant,
Oh! what a day I've had
I'm not afraid of giants,

'Cause this giant is my dad.

David Whitehead

My Bed

My bed is like a little boat
floating out to sea.
And now it's like an island
with a coconut tree.

My bed is like a racing car
roaring in a race.
And now it's like a rocket
rising into space.

My bed is like a submarine
diving down deep.
But now my bed is just a bed
because I'm going to sleep.

Tony Mitton

KNOWSLEY SCHOOL LIBRARY SERVICE PROJECT LOAN